Castle

A Social History

PUBLISHED BY THE LARKS PRESS
Ordnance Farmhouse, Guist Bottom,
Dereham, Norfolk NR20 5PF

01328 829207

IN ASSOCIATION WITH BEAGLE PUBLISHING
Fiddlers Green, Castle Acre,
King's Lynn PE32 2BT

Printed by the Witley Press, Hunstanton, Norfolk
March 2009

© Mary-Anne Garry

British Library Cataloguing-in-Publication Data
*A catalogue record for this book is available
from the British Library*

ISBN 978 1904006 46 6

Castle Acre

A Social History

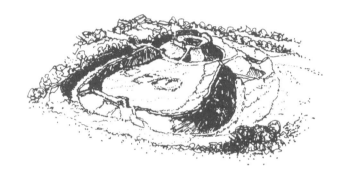

MARY-ANNE GARRY

THE LARKS PRESS

in association with

BEAGLE PUBLISHING

ACKNOWLEDGEMENTS

The author would like to thank the following people for their help with the production of this book:

The Earl of Leicester and Lord Coke for allowing access to the Holkham archives, and Christine Hiskey the archivist there;

Helen Breach for the cover picture, the map and other illustrations inside;

the late Syd Davison for his drawings of village houses;

Joan Matthews for the design of the book and her great care in preparing it for the printers;

also Jean Joice, Robert Liddiard, Tom North, Carole Rawcliffe, Robert Rickett, Rachel Young and lastly Sonia Warnes for allowing me to use her research on the council housing in Town Lane.

FOREWORD

THIS BOOK has grown from a few lines of history by way of introduction to the Village Guide of the 1980s to its present form. An earlier edition, published in 2001, had the Village Guide and Map printed on separate sheets and tucked in at the back of the book. The constantly changing state of village amenities made it difficult to keep the Guide up-to-date and it was decided in 2008 to create a website which could be corrected more easily. Village information can now be found at www.castleacre.info. From a historian's viewpoint Castle Acre enjoys the immense advantage that from 1616 the majority of the parish was owned by the Coke family of Holkham, whose archives are a treasure trove. The Earl of Leicester has allowed me to spend many hours at Holkham and this book is one result of my researches there. The aim was to record how people lived in the village, as the history and architecture of the Castle and Priory is covered by the English Heritage Guide. A thousand years of history in one small book inevitably means that only the tip of the iceberg has been uncovered –twenty-seven closely written volumes would probably be needed to do it justice. My particular interest is the eighteenth century; should anyone wish to know more about Castle Acre during that period, I might be able to answer their enquiries.

In 2001 the book was sold to raise money for a new children's playground which has long since been created on the Playing Fields. All those involved in the production of the book gave their services and talents free of charge, for which I am truly appreciative. The book continues to be a non-profit making venture; proceeds go towards printing the next edition.

MARY-ANNE GARRY
March 2009

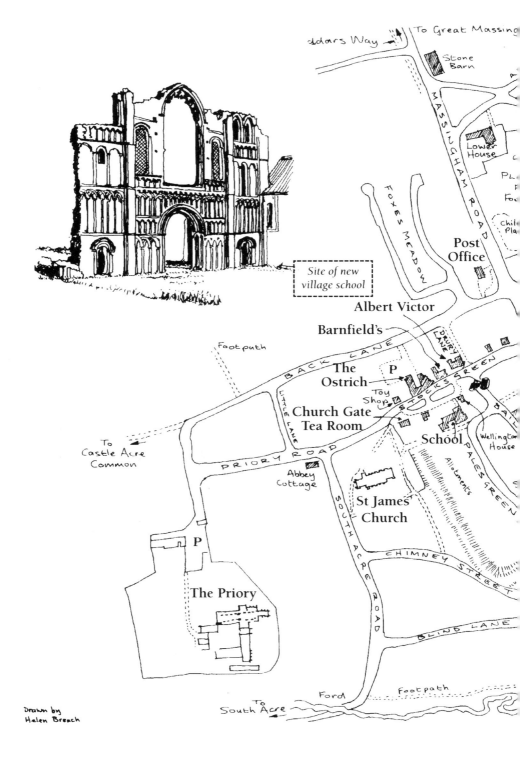

To Great Massing

ddars Way

Stone Barn

MASSINGHAM ROAD

Lower House

PL

Fo

Chi
Pla

Post Office

FOXES MEADOW

Site of new village school

Albert Victor

Barnfield's

DRURY LANE

STOCKS GREEN

BACK LANE

The Ostrich

P

Toy Shop

BALL

Footpath

LITTLE LANE

Church Gate Tea Room

School

Wellington House

To Castle Acre Common

PRIORY ROAD

Abbey Cottage

PALES GREEN

Allotments

SOUTH ACRE ROAD

St James Church

P

The Priory

CHIMNEY STREET

BLIND LANE

Ford

Footpath

To South Acre

Drawn by Helen Breach

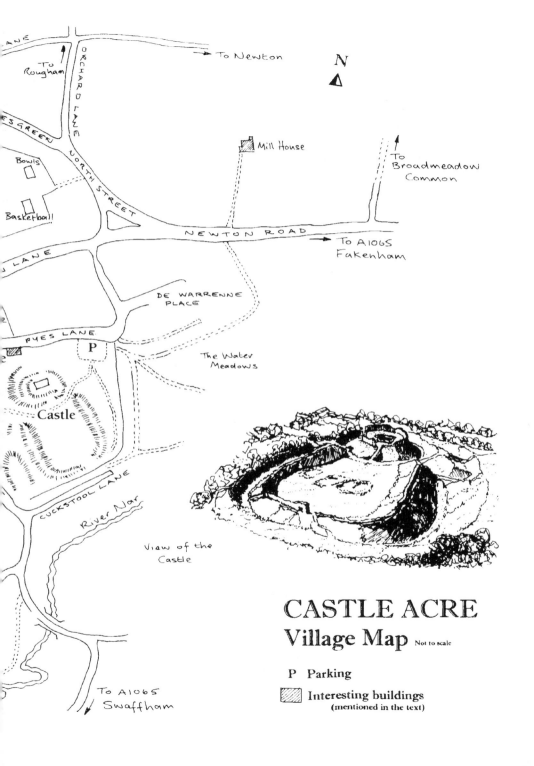

CASTLE ACRE
Village Map <small>Not to scale</small>

P   Parking

Interesting buildings
(mentioned in the text)

1 The Normans make their Mark

CASTLE ACRE is a rural village in north west Norfolk; it lies four miles north of Swaffham to the west of the A1065 at the point where the river Nar is crossed by an ancient route known as the Peddars Way.

The Peddars Way stretches for approximately forty-six miles, from near Ixworth in Suffolk to north Norfolk. The discovery of Seahenge at Holme-next-the-Sea, now on display in Lynn Museum, suggest this may have been the goal of the path, though its exact purpose remains unknown. It is thought to pre-date the Romans who paved it, and today is a popular walk for the very reason that it is rural: Castle Acre is one of the few villages on its route. The parish of Castle Acre is pearshaped; the Peddars Way enters at the southern-most point, runs northwards through the village and beyond to the furthest tip in the north, as though reluctant to leave. Here it crosses the old east-west route from King's Lynn to Norwich, and from there on borders a further six or more parishes, though without entering them, before reaching the coast.

The river Nar, on the other hand, is less of a mystery: it rises near Mileham and flows west for twenty-six miles to the river Ouse at King's Lynn. Altered over the years to provide navigable straits down stream from West Acre, 'floated' water meadows at Castle Acre and a pleasure pond at Lexham, it is essentially a chalk-based trout stream of high quality and largely unpolluted by chemicals.

Numerous finds of the Palaeolithic and Neolithic period have been discovered in the area but little to suggest a Roman settlement, nothing more than some scattered Romano-British coins and pottery fragments; no villa such as that at Weasenham five miles to the north or Gayton Thorpe equidistant to the west. There is some evidence of

Roman farming, mixed cereal crops.

The Anglo-Saxons left a cemetery on the western border of the parish which, when ploughed in 1961, revealed many fragments of cremation-urns, grave goods and bones. During the final years of the Saxon period, immediately prior to the coming of the Normans in 1066, Toki was the lord in Castle Acre, one among many manors he owned throughout East Anglia. By this date parish boundaries had been established with tithes payable to the priests, though later in the thirteenth century they were to be formalised by the church, and in the nineteenth century by the civil authorities.

The river dominated the valley: meadows for grazing on each bank, and fields and settlements behind. Toki may well have had his house on the site of the castle, surrounded by the villagers who we know grew peas, beans, carrots, celery and fruit. Some goats were kept and there were horses but these were not yet used to pull ploughs. At the Domesday count Toki's settlement of 'Acre' had six horses, eight oxen, forty-five swine, a hundred and sixty sheep and two ploughs; the unusually large number of swine suggests a good bit of woodland nearby. There were two hundred and twenty-eight people in the village, some of whom owned their own land. The Priory's charter tells us in 1087 that the land between the castle and the site of the Priory was orchard, very possibly of long standing, which might be a clue to the village name, since Acre means field.

With the advent of the Normans Toki's lands were given to William de Warenne for his part in the Battle of Hastings; de Warenne was one of the few men who can be shown to have crossed the channel with William the Conqueror in 1066. Legend has it that he married William the Conqueror's daughter, but it is more likely that Gundrada was the child of the Earl of Chester. In 1070 Frederic, the brother of de Warenne's soon-to-be wife, was killed fighting Hereward the Wake in

Bailey Street: looking north towards the Bailey Gate

the Fens and Frederic's lands in Norfolk, another nineteen manors including South Acre and Lexham, passed to de Warenne.

In all he held land in thirteen English counties in 1086, notably Lewes in Sussex, Reigate in Surrey and Conisburgh in Yorkshire, where he also built castles. The de Warenne family were effective land managers and while many another well rewarded Domesday family went rapidly downhill the de Warennes stayed up. Shortly before his death at the siege of Pevensey in 1088 William de Warenne was created Earl of Surrey.

The castle at Castle Acre was built less as a fortress and more as a high status country house; the Norman conquerors wished to show who was in charge and what sort of building was suitable for people of their kind: a stone one. However, as Toki had also been a great lord

11

in his time there is a strong suspicion that the pre-Norman ramparts beneath the bailey banks are of Late Saxon date, so that in many respects the early Norman manor house may have been similar to that of Toki's. Going further back still some believe that the south-facing earthworks date to Neolithic times.

More can be read about the architecture and structure of the castle in the English Heritage guide, but it is worth noting that it was built by local muscle, using local flint faced with Barnack stone brought upstream by flat-bottomed barges.

Somewhat later after the bailey, outer bailey and barbican were dug out and, in about 1200, the great Gate, now known erroneously as the Bailey Gate, was built at the north end of the main street. This was part of a larger earthwork enclosing Bailey Street, the castle and what is now Pales Green, at that time not yet built upon. This has been described as a planned town, but as it consisted of no more than one street this is hard to substantiate. What it did enclose was the slightly altered route of the Peddars Way; originally it had skirted the settlement, but was now re-directed in line with the castle. Travellers were obliged to pay a toll to cross the river, where a Stone Bridge was built for foot passengers. The name Toll House Green was given to the area behind what is today the Old Red Lion in Bailey Street, at the western entrance to the castle. The castle was thus in control of the river and the roads, which took on a further importance when the shrine of Walsingham was built in the early twelfth century and became second only in popularity to Canterbury as a pilgrim destination.

When William de Warenne died in 1088, he was succeeded by his son the second earl, also William, who lived mainly on the de Warenne estates in Normandy, though possibly he founded the Priory, perhaps at the time of his marriage in 1118. His son William, the third earl, was a soldier. He spent time in England and may have been responsible for fortifying the castle during turbulent times when taking the side of King Stephen against Matilda; he fought at the battle of Lincoln in 1141. In 1146 he set out on a crusade but did not return; he reached Syria the following year, only to be killed there by the Turks.

Subsequently another Earl William is known to have been at Castle Acre when Henry III visited, more than once, probably on his way to Walsingham. His son John likewise entertained Edward I here. This John's grandson, the last of the de Warennes, had a complicated love life as a result of which he forfeited but eventually regained the castle, dying without an heir in 1347.

The castle was one of the finer Norman country houses, sizeable and sophisticated in a fairly peaceful area. Had the keep ever been completed it would have been very imposing and majestic, especially on the southern approaches. Numerous finds, many now in the Castle Museum, Norwich, include fine personal adornments, pendants, rings, brooches, and metalwork fittings, including hinges and padlocks. There is also evidence of musical instruments, mainly pipes, and counters for games, dice and Nine Mens Morris. One of the most important finds was the arm of a coin-checking balance, the earliest and most elaborate English example. All these together with dietary remains, bones of deer, rabbits and game, ducks, geese, partridge, and swans, the seeds of oats, barley, wheat and rye, point to wealth.

As well as controlling the river and the Peddars Way the Lord of the Manor also had charge of the village water mills. Castle Acre was divided into three manors known as Arundells (they were to inherit the castle), Priors for the Priory and Foxes. Foxes, which lay mainly to the north and east of the village, also encompassed the main public

SYD DAVISON

*The Mill at Newton Common, the last of the three mills
in use until the mid-twentieth century*

house, now the Ostrich, and held the tolls from the Fairs. Almost from its inception the Priory held the three water mills; the first was within the grounds of the Priory. The second was the Mill-in-the-Hole, the site of which is the meadow across the river from the castle and can be seen as a hollowing out. This mill has long since gone and more recently the area has been known as the Little Winds. The river was altered in the nineteenth century when an experiment was carried out to form 'floated' water meadows; as a consequence it no longer flows past the site of the old mill but in an unnatural straight line. For those who walk there the original bed of the river is easy to see, not least because of the numerous springs that dance out of the ground. Prior to the diversion the river opened out into a pond before it reached the Stone Bridge, known as the Earl's Pond, adjacent to the 'Lawndry House' at the foot of the castle. The strip of land known as Cuckstool

Lane, on the north side of the river, was common or waste ground, allowing access to the Mill-in-the-Hole. Both mills had fallen into disuse by the late seventeenth century. The third mill still stands today further upstream where it straddles the river at Newton Common. The parish boundary of Castle Acre is careful to cross the water and take in land on the other side; where the mills are involved, the river is only used as a demarcation when it is of no disadvantage to lose the further bank.

The foundation charter needed to form a Priory is dated 1087-1089 when William and Gundrada were both still alive. They chose monks of the Cluniac order, the same as they had on another of their estates at Lewes in Sussex, some of whom were already 'in the church of our castle of Acre' suggesting a castle chapel within the bailey as at Castle Rising. The charter was renewed by the second earl circa 1110 and from this we know that the monks established in the castle had already begun the Priory on the present site. The second earl gave them 'two orchards and all the cultivated ground from the orchards to my castle, which by my encouragement and help they have now founded their church, because that in which they now dwell is too strait and inconvenient for an abode of monks.' He also gave them his serf, Ulmar, the stonemason. The Priory church and buildings were built in the lifetime of the third earl between 1146 and 1148 and con-secrated by William Turbus, Bishop of Norwich. The second earl saw to it that it was generously endowed from the beginning. He gave the churches of Castle Acre, Methwold, Trunch and Leaden Roding in Essex and two parts of his demesnes in Grimstone in Norfolk. These were added to by subsequent Kings and nobles so that by 1291 the possessions were extensive, in seventy-eight Norfolk parishes and two in Suffolk and Lincoln. It had four daughter houses and a dependant

15

leper hospital at South Acre with a church or chapel there dedicated to St Bartholomew. Although the tithes and profits of the Priory were due to the Abbot of Cluny, from 1295 war with France provided a handy impediment. However this led to complications: if the French were not to profit, then why not the English? Edward I demanded they were paid to the exchequer. After some time it was argued that they were by now completely English and no longer bound by the Abbot of Cluny (who did not agree), but it was not until 1373 that Castle Acre and other Cluniac houses were naturalised. By this date monasteries were beginning to lose their appeal; very few new ones were built and gradually they ceased to be regarded as centres of excellence for learning and models of community life. It became more difficult to endow a monastery or nunnery after 1279 when the Statute of Mortmain made it illegal to grant land to a corporation without specific permission from the Crown, which was difficult and expensive to obtain. Religious houses were beginning to be seen as simply great land-owning establishments and commercial centres. Further, Cluniacs were an enclosed order: they did not mix with the villagers, offer them education or preach or minister to them; the infirmaries in the Priory were exclusively for the monks. Their one concession was the possible existence of an almshouse near the gates. However, they were obliged by law to provide free overnight shelter for travellers and at the Dissolution of the Monasteries the person who bought the monastic site and buildings was supposed to go on doing this, often retaining the gate house for the purpose. The Tudor gate house at the Priory is evidence of this.

Many grand and monied people paid to be buried in the chancel of the great church, with the monks to pray for their souls *in perpetuam,* but apart from this their lives were secretive; very few visitors penetrated even the outer gates. The monks collected tithes, controlled the mills and farmed large areas of the parish, their sheep walks centred around Monk's Wicken; but in order to comply with their enclosed life in the priory most of this activity would have been carried out by sub-tenants, who in turn employed villagers.

2 The Monks depart

WITH THE departure of the last de Warenne from the castle in 1347 life at the Priory also went down hill. Numbers had been falling for some time, from fifty to thirty, and now in 1351 the King had to instruct his sergeant-at-arms to arrest some of the monks who had 'spurned the habit of their order and were vagabonds in England in secular habit'. They were duly punished. Bad publicity where secrecy is involved is always recorded and remembered. A few snippets from the time show that windmills appeared to compete with the water mills, and then small handmills, which were forbidden; the court records are full of seizures and fines for their use. In 1309 Margaret Garhole was brought before the court (held in the public house) and accused of 'harbouring two maid servants who habitually gleaned wrongfully and carried away the grain of the earl and the neighbours in autumn.' Held responsible, she was fined sixpence. This type of agricultural misdemeanour does not change greatly over the years. Three crimes touching Castle Acre are recorded for the year 1316: the first involved a cow stolen from Saham Toney near Watton and sold at Castle Acre market; the second a Castle Acre man, John of Woodland, burgled the house of Sarah, former wife of Thomas, son of Peter of Lexham, at night and stole goods to the value of forty shillings. A considerable amount, and he paid dearly for it – he was hanged. The third is a murder: Agnes of Acre robbed a merchant of his linen, woollen cloth and his horse, worth together £10, at Stratford Attebowe (London) and then killed him. Note the absence of surnames and the serious nature of the crimes.

In November 1537, over two hundred years later, Prior Thomas Malling surrendered the Priory to the Crown. By then the monks had

The Parish Church of St. James the Great

been reduced in number to ten and five lay brothers.

As with the castle, the English Heritage guide describes the fabric and building of the Priory.

The effect of the dissolution of the Priory and the dispersal of the monks, the burning of books and manuscripts, although never before seen by the inhabitants of Castle Acre, would have shocked the village. Religious houses were abolished and their lands reverted to the Crown for economic not religious reasons. Until the death of Henry VIII on January 28 1547 England remained a Catholic country, but Catholic without the Pope. Protestants were burnt as heretics throughout his reign and Catholics beliefs enforced with savage penalties. Henry wanted money to make war on France and finance an extravagant lifestyle; religious houses had been closed before to raise money – for

19

instance by Henry V and by Cardinal Wolsey – but never all of them at once, as now. Henry had also planned to abolish religious guilds and chantries, hospitals and colleges; this was done during the reign of Edward VI. Records show there were at least two guildhalls, albeit small, in Castle Acre.

It was not until the reign of the boy King Edward VI that England became Protestant, only to revert to Catholicism under Mary.

The parish church also changed from the old faith to the new. The priest in 1506 was William Stephenson, according to Blomefield the Norfolk historian. His successor Robert Pepper was appointed by King Edward in 1550. Two possible scenarios here: one is that Stephenson changed his faith and stayed to 1550, another that turbulent times ensued and matters were not straightened out until Pepper was appointed.

Economically the village appears to have suffered very little. Henry VIII had already closed down the shrines and confiscated their wealth before he began on the religious houses; neither religious houses nor pilgrimages (both declining in popularity) were core items of the Catholic faith. There were fewer and fewer pilgrims paying handsomely to sleep on straw-filled mattresses on their way to Walsingham.

An annual fair held on St James's Day July 25 dates back to at least 1275, probably earlier, and was held on St James's Fairstead (Green), a large area at the north of the village, the church green, or as it is now called Stocks Green, being too small. This indicates good trade, and was the main medieval fair surviving into the nineteenth century. A second fair was held on May 1, the feast of SS Philip and James the Less. Charters confirming the markets survive from the late fourteenth century.

Further evidence of the village being a wealthy place in the four-teenth century can be seen by looking at the parish church. The present building, which is a large one even by East Anglian standards, reflects this. Inside, the high quality of painting is still visible today on the pulpit and rood screen, which both date from circa 1400. Thirty acres of glebe land went with the church and a vicarage was built in the field immediately to the south, a house which has long since dis-appeared without trace. Traditionally most village business was carried out in the south porch of the church so it was an advantage for the vicar to live within view.

Castle Acre had always had its share of prosperous inhabitants, as may be seen in a rental of 1474 and the number of those who made wills. Wills were only made by those who had property to leave. John Fox, for whom Foxes Manor was named, died in 1465 and held lands in Congham, Barwick, Castle Acre, Newton and Lexham. He was rich enough to leave £40 each to his two children besides silver spoons and some plate; to his wife Katherine he left his hundred best ewes and four best horses. In addition he left handsome amounts to the Priory, and to his servants. (It was common to own land in different parishes.)

The Callybut family who succeeded the Foxes were richer still and paid for the south aisle of the church to be built. A memorial stone in what was known as Callybut's chapel records the death of Margerie wife of Francis Callybut who died in 1515. Unfortunately this, along with many others, was covered up by Victorian tiles in the great refurbishment of 1858.

Henry Scotting, who died in 1525 and was buried in the Lady Chapel of the church, is typical of the next sort of man down. He owned three houses in the village, one of which was an alehouse, and another house at Newton, plus land. He left donations to the Greyfriars and Carmelites at Norwich and the Blackfriars and Austins at Lynn, money to repair the churches of Castle Acre and Newton and to a priest to sing at Castle Acre for a year for the repose of his soul. A prosperous but pious man.

Thirty years later in 1552, after the dissolution and with John Pepper the first Protestant vicar of the church, Henry Scotting's son John is churchwarden and certifies that 'with the consent of the whole town' they have agreed to sell an old cross for ten pounds, which will pay for the whiting of the church and the mending of the windows.

Whitewashing the church was to cover the wall paintings and decorations of the old faith, while 'mending the windows' suggests they may have been broken in order to destroy the religious pictures in the glass. An act of Parliament passed that same year 1552 ordered superstitious ornaments to be destroyed or defaced and 'superfluous' church goods sold and the money given to the Crown, leaving a church one chalice and one bell. The extent to which the Act was carried out varied from church to church.

According to Blomefield, 'Old Paine of Castle Acre was standard bearer to Henry VIII and had a daughter who was married and widowed three times.' Certainly Old Mistress Guybon was resident at the Priory in 1616, the widow of Anthony Hoogan, James Audley and Humphrey Guybon, all of whom were buried in the chancel of the parish church.

An important fact regarding land ownership in Castle Acre was the co-existence of both freehold and copyhold properties. While the Lords of the three manors between them either owned most of the land or had copyhold rights over it, there has always been a substantial amount that was freehold. Henry Scotting, for example, held land free of the lord. Each time a copyhold property, either land or a building, changed ownership either by inheritance or purchase, the transaction was recorded in the Court Rolls, which in the case of Castle Acre go back to 1200. A court was held annually in the village, sometimes twice a year, to record these changes and administer small judgements, such as the aforementioned Margaret Garhole and her gleaning maids, and to settle minor disputes.

Freehold properties had title deeds, needed to prove ownership, but these were left to the individual to keep in the safest place he or she knew, and were not entered in the Court Rolls. Many such documents have been thrown away over the years as with each change of ownership more and more were accumulated; this makes it relatively easy to trace a copyhold property but it can be frustratingly difficult for those that were held 'Free of the Manor.' Added to which houses exist in Castle Acre today where once there were none, and equally houses once stood where now there are only gardens and fields.

The Court Rolls were written in Latin until 1733 and go to some trouble to describe the exact position of the copyhold properties, abutting north, south, east and west on their neighbours. There were no maps or plans. The presence of so many freehold properties in the village meant the village was unlikely ever to be owned by one person –it was never an estate village– but an open one. A significant percentage of houses and acreage remained independently owned, and this was to become an important factor in the nineteenth century.

Therefore the rental drawn up for Lady Anne Gresham in 1582, widow of Sir Thomas Gresham who had acquired the Manors of Priors and Arundells after the dissolution, which covers all three manors both free and copyhold, is extremely valuable. Sir Thomas Gresham a London merchant owned large tracts of ex-ecclesiastical lands; Castle Acre was but one of many. Being the right age at the right time, in this case in the 1540s, saw the foundation of many a land-owning family. However Gresham had no heir.

By 1582 there were eighty-eight houses in the village, a little less than a third of today's number, of which seventeen were empty. The castle had been uninhabited for many years, its slopes and ditches grazed by cattle and sheep. The large stones which can be seen in the foundations of several cottages and houses in the village would have been in place by this date: many of them clearly originate from the Priory, some houses have whole stone quoins. Possibly it was 'lucky' as well as practical to have a souvenir of the old days. Stone from many religious houses was sold at the time of the dissolution, or else broken up and used to improve the roads. Castle Acre Priory is an extensive complex, though by no means all of it would have been stone clad.

The rental does not help us to know how many people lived in the village, for there were always those who owned houses and land and lived elsewhere. So the number of non-property-owning inhabitants can only be guessed at. However the names of the houses are recorded and are usually named for those who built them. The outline shape of the village was the same as it is today, though the majority of the houses would have been single storey with steeply sloping thatched roofs. Examples of these can be seen by looking at the gable ends of houses. Wellington House on Stocks Green, though later in date, shows how the roof line has been altered over the years. Upgreen was St James's Green and here Lady Bell owned a large house near to the present Stone Barn, which was to become the farm house for the eastern part of the parish, eventually Lodge Farm. Opposite, on the south side of the Green, John Wingfield owned Blanches, now Lower House. The Grove at the east end of Stocks Green before it was rebuilt at the beginning of the twentieth century had been known in earlier times as Candishes after Richard Candishe who died in 1519. Anthony Pettifer lived in what is probably the most important surviving house in the village now called Tudor Lodgings at the south end of Pales Green. Pettifer called it Hennings. Stocks Green, the centre of the village, was known as Markett Street and at this date, although there were buildings on the north side, there were none on the south side, suggesting that some form of earthwork or ditch still survived. Hugh Wood was the landlord of the pub then called the Crown (now the Ostrich, the emblem of the Coke family), where the one village shop was located. One shop may not seem like much but for 1582 it was rather go-ahead to have one at all; most shopping was done at market. The Scotting family had a pub called The Bull on the corner of Drury Lane east, then called Mussellboroughe or Muckleburrow Lane, and to the west was another called Ye Old Swann. The present café and

Looking east down the High Street with The Grove at the end,
formerly called Candishes

25

stores currently called Barnfields and the Albert Victor pub, both free-hold properties, were residential dwellings in 1582. Many place names are the same then as now: Bailey Street, Cuckstool Common and East Green. Chimney Street appears at this date, though the origin of the name is as yet unclear. In Bailey Street there was a house near the entrance to the castle 'le guildhalle, almost ruined.' The small cottage in the north-east corner of the Priory grounds with the blocked east window may have been a chapel or the second guildhall; its origins are unclear.

One of the water mills was already out of use, the two remaining ones were run by one man, John Mower, who in 1577 had been granted a twenty-one year lease for them. In keeping with the best romantic traditions he had no sons, but three daughters.

Anthony Huggon, Gent., lived in what is described as the one 'well and sufficiently built … mansion house, spacious and agreeable for lodgings for one gentleman' namely the Priory. The rental describes it as 'the late Monastery of Castleacre' with its saffron grounds, barns, and malting house. Soon it was to be known as Abbey Farm and would be home to the 'capital' or most important farmer in the parish.

3 Secular Landlords and National Conflict

IN JUNE 1583 Lady Anne Gresham sold her manors in Castle Acre along with others she owned in West Acre, Mileham and Beeston, to Sir Thomas Cecil, the eldest son of William Cecil, Queen Elizabeth's High Treasurer. In 1616 Sir Edward Coke of Mileham purchased the Manors of Priors and Arundells from his brother-in law William Cecil, Thomas's son. There is a story that the extent of Sir Edward's land purchases worried King James, but when he heard about Castle Acre he was soothed on being told that it was but 'one more acre.' Sir Edward was not an especially avaricious man when it came to landownership so the tale is most likely to be apocryphal. In 1616 he was out of favour at court and with time on his hands the possibility of restoring the ruined castle seems to have been, momentarily, an actual project. A bill survives for repairs to the walls and a turret, done at his 'express commands, the finishing up of eleven battlements and mason's work' but no sooner had this work been carried out than the tide turned and he was summoned back to court. Sir Edward lived mainly in London and at a house at Stoke Poges, Buckinghamshire; he was the Lord Chief Justice for much of his career.

At about the same time the Manor of Foxes changed ownership: in 1576, after the Callybuts had failed to produce a male heir, the four daughters sold out to Robert Bell of Outwell, who in turn sold it to a Castle Acre man, Mr Gay. In 1611 Sir Edward Coke's steward, who already owned land at Godwick near Tittleshall, bought Foxes Manor for £1,820.

Moving into the seventeenth century, the Court Rolls of 1626 repeat the usual village problems; those that could not be solved privately often involve people from neighbouring parishes. Anthony Killingworth of Westacre probably lived even further away: his house on Stocks Green was falling down and he had failed to scour his ditch to the great nuisance of everyone else and as this was against the law he was fined 3d and told he must put it to rights by the following month. Edward Barkham, the Lord of the Manor of Southacre and sometime Lord Mayor of London, was taken to task for having unlawfully enclosed a certain way called 'a drifte way' used by cattle and carriages. The Town of West Lexham is in trouble at every single court for allowing their cattle and sheep to stray onto Manuels Common and graze there. Every year without fail they are fined and every single year they fail to pay up. By the end of the century they must have owed Castle Acre at least a hundred pounds, and still do to this day.

Thomas Chapman and Richard Dowing were fined 3d for laying and making muck in the street of Castle Acre being a great nuisance to the people and if they do it again they will be fined 8d. Everyone is reminded that it is an offence to take flaggs from the commons and sell them. These crimes are constantly repeated despite the fines. Illegal grazing and leaving muck in the streets are the most common.

The river was a further source of dispute. In 1663 Edward Tye was charged with not looking after it as had been agreed; he was told to get on with it and fined 12d. He was to keep it clean between the Stone Bridge and South Acre bridge. The Stone Bridge was mentioned in the rental of 1582 but was probably constructed long before. There is no record of what the present bridge, built at the time of Queen Victoria's Jubilee in 1897, replaced but it was probably a footbridge with the ford beside it.

Two constables were appointed to deal with disputes between inhabitants and two pinders to deal with the animals. These men were given two pence for every swine (pig) they found roaming 'in the town

CASTLEACRE COMMONS.

NOTICE to Owners of Stock and others Utilizing the above Commons.

The Castleacre Commons Committee have decided to RE-OPEN the Commons on   next ensuing.

ALL STOCK must be paid for **BEFORE BEING TURNED UPON THE COMMONS,** otherwise they will be liable to be impounded. **PASSES** in accordance with the following Scale of charges can be obtained of the Collector—MR. WALTER HOWARD, St. JAMES GREEN, Castleacre.

	Per Year or part thereof s. d.		s. d.
For every Horse	5 0	Mule	5 0
Mare and Foal	7 6	Donkey	4 0
Cow	5 0	Donkey and Foal	5 0
Cow and Calf	7 6	Goat	2 6
Bullock	5 0	Sheep	2 6
		Geese and Goslings (Per Head)	3

The Committee has authorized the above named Collector to sell any person "a Bargain" of Rushes for 1/- (a Bargain being an ordinary Cart Load) the Collector to use his own discretion in the matter, and no person to be allowed to purchase more than two "Bargains" otherwise, no person is to take Flag, Sedge, Rushes, or Dung, from the Commons.

The Committee cannot be responsible for Damage to Stock or for Straying,

By Order of the Castleacre Commons Committee.

F. A. TAYLOR,

Chairman.

Early twentieth-century grazing charges for animals on the commons

and ringing the same'. Those whose swine were not ringed were fined. Swine were supposed to be ringed by October 20 after which date they would be deemed to be trespassing. Further, any cattle or beast belonging to any person in the town of Castle Acre found damaging the ground belonging to another after March 20 each year, when seeds had been sown and were starting to shoot, would be taken into the pound and the owner fined four shillings. These were hefty charges: the authorities probably considered that, given the amount of common land available in the parish for grazing, the owners had no excuse to break the rules. Those that trespassed on a field in harvest time '[before] three days after the corne shall be taken off' were in even more serious trouble. There were also strict rules for people daring to rake either 'with a long or a short rake upon any manor lands in the tyme of harvest' without permission.

It was in the seventeenth century that two charities were set up to benefit the poor of Castle Acre: in his will of 1629 William Allen of East Lexham bequeathed them thirty-two shillings a year, and Mr Coney of Southacre ten shillings. These charities survived until quite recently with the interest paid to the civil Parish Council, by which time the administration costs far exceeded their worth.

The three main commons, Manuels (so often invaded by Lexhamites), Broadmeadow and the common that stretches to Westacre were never enclosed. Thanks to the river they were too marshy to plough up and within living memory were objects of pride, closely grazed by a variety of stock from geese to donkeys. They cover about thirty-two acres. In earlier times animals were collected daily from their different owners and driven to the commons, returning each evening. Prior to the eighteenth century there had been another large common in the north of the parish.

By 1689 the problem of keeping the river clear of weeds became so acute that a resolution was passed: on the second Thursday in June for the next seven years labourers were to be sent by the farmers and others to cut and clear the water course, risking a two shilling fine for not complying. Perennial problems are a feature of most villages; in the twenty-first century it is car parking.

Larger conflicts such as the Civil War in the middle of the seventeenth century merit no mention in the business of the village and in the same way the Parish Council minutes make not one reference to the 1914-18 war a hundred and sixty years later. Yet both had a huge impact. In the Civil War potentially everyone was affected as working men were conscripted by both sides.

Henry Beck's son Jeremy was now Lord of the Manor of Foxes. At the outbreak he was a young man studying law at the Inner Temple in London. His father had recently died and he had inherited substantial property, not just in Castle Acre but also in Suffolk. Though not an active Royalist he had gone into King's Lynn at the time of the Royalist coup in the summer of 1643, which was seen as evidence enough to judge his sympathies and he was committed to Lambeth House in September 1644, charged with threatening officers. His estates were sequestrated and it was only after 1650 that he was able to redeem them at a cost; he was obliged to sell the land in Suffolk to pay his fine.

The Mayor of Lynn in 1643-4 was Edmund Hudson, a Castle Acre man and probably a Royalist, though it is unclear to what extent he was manipulated by the royalist gentry. His family had held land in the parish since at least 1604, a house called Blabbes on the south side of Chimney Street (now a field) and other land, though he may have lived principally in King's Lynn. Like many, Edmund Hudson had diverse interests; he is described in the Court Rolls as a woollen draper; he married Mary, the daughter of Edward Barkham, Lord of the Manor of Southacre. After the death of John Percival in 1644 the freemen of Lynn tried to elect Hudson as their M.P. but this failed, as he was still disqualified from sitting for 'having assisted at the rising of Lynn.'

On the Parliamentary side it is supposed that Oliver Cromwell's mother, a Norfolk woman, had family in Swaffham, the Stewards, while West Lexham was the birthplace of Philip Skippon, General in the Parliamentary Army and the head of the London militia.

Recent research has shown that almost every person in the land was obliged to take sides, even if passive, during what the eighteenth-century vicar of Castle Acre called The Great Rebellion. There must have been many 'warm words at the tavern at the Sign of the Ostrich' which the Crown pub was now named.

Superficially stability marks the seventeenth century in Castle Acre but the effect of the Civil War should not be underestimated and may account for the tithe books which show the vicar receiving hearthtax (a nominal charge of one penny) and tithes from a hundred and seven households in the parish in 1644, an increase of twenty-nine houses since 1582; whereas the year before, 1643, he had only managed to get eighty-nine households to comply. Tithes paid to the church were in kind: a roasting pig, a bushel of apples, honey, eggs, wool –whatever could be procured– and the balancing and collection of them, being fair to all parties, took up an inordinate amount of time, even when a clerk was employed to help out. Accusations of cheating and con-spiracy were as common as complaints about unringed swine and muck on the roads. Poorly paid by their masters, the Church of England, the clergy must have longed to receive their tithes in coins, but geese, ducks, beans, hemp and such like was one of the few unbroken traditions reaching back to before the Conquest. Bartering still played a large part in village life and as people set up their stalls on the market their goods were more likely to be exchanged than paid for in cash. Many had quite small tables offering just a few items, such as one sees today in the Third World.

By the end of the seventeenth century the rural sector of the parish was still divided into the three main fields that roughly, but only very roughly, went with the three manors: West Field, largely sheep walks, Middle Field and East Field. Strip farming was still practised, hence the care over animals that strayed since there were no fences. Considerable numbers of strips, intermixed with Holkham land, were owned by families descended from the Scottings, Hudsons, Gays and others, the majority in the West Field and along what is now Back Lane and its hinterland.

4 Holkham's Investment – Agricultural Improvements

THE EIGHTEENTH century was to see this change. From Holkham, now the principal seat of the Coke family, the four guardians of young Thomas Coke from 1707-18 began a systematic agricultural reform which was continued by Thomas and his descendants. They started by reviewing the rents, which had stayed unchanged throughout the seventeenth century, even decreasing a little in some parishes. To improve the revenue of their tenant farmers and justify rent increases, it was planned to buy up any strips of farmland 'intermingled with Mr Coke's' which would then be measured out into smaller fields bordered by hedges, ploughed and spread with marl, dug from a pit usually sunk in the middle of the field. These pits were circled by trees, often beech, and can still be seen. Marl, a clay- like substance, was beneficial to the light soils of the area when used as a top dressing. The Guardians allocated money towards improvements in farm buildings and farm houses; fortuitously a severe gale in 1713 flattened several of the more shaky barns and new ones were built to replace them. In Castle Acre a Holkham man, Francis Anderson, was given the tenancy of the Abbey Farm and overall charge of the parish, an unofficial lord of the manor. The manor of Foxes was purchased from Beck's descendants by Holkham in 1714 and Anderson, who already had the water mill under his jurisdiction, was given the Ostrich pub with its adjoining small farm, and the tolls of the Fairs.

At Newton the old mill had burnt down in the 1680s and been rebuilt, but in 1710 the roof fell in and large sections of the building were replaced. The rebuilding in the seventeenth century must have been of a poor standard, for in the storm of 1713 more damage was done 'the groundwork being decayed.' The mill remained under the control of Francis Anderson until 1727. There were other mills, windmills, in the village and at Newton, though no record of where precisely. Later there was a smock mill in Sandy Lane by the Broadmeadow Common and later still at Mill House.

As the transformation of the fields progressed thousands of layers were brought to plant hedges, many of which still survive dividing the fields. If you walk down the hedges and count the layers you may often find that a hedge is a hundred layers long. Increased digging, layering, ploughing, weeding and marling meant an increased work force. Most were day labourers with a reasonable security of employment; ideally their wives and daughters remained at home spinning and tending livestock. For those who could afford to buy an animal there was always grazing to be had on the commons.

The Albert Victor public house

Was life in eighteenth-century Castle Acre therefore an idyll? Almost certainly not for the poorest: very few labouring families survive from one generation to the next in the parish registers, where the name of the person is followed by the description 'a poor man'. Craftsmen, bakers, carpenters, shoemakers and others, many of whom followed more than one trade, were more likely to settle and buy a house. What has often surprised students of Castle Acre history is how so many trades and craftsmen managed to survive and thrive only four miles from Swaffham. Until recently the same question could still have been posed: when the first edition of this book was written in 2001 there were seven shops in the village, but as this current edition goes to press in 2009 the number has dwindled considerably. Even so, in part thanks to tourists, Castle Acre continues to support some businesses when in many surrounding villages at a much greater distance from Swaffham there are none, and in some cases not even a pub.

5 Pimlowe the vicar – living with the Church of England

IN 1709 the old vicar the Rev. Briggs died. His successor was to be a young newly-inducted man, Ambrose Pimlowe, vicar of Rougham, an adjoining parish, who had arrived there only months earlier. Previously Pimlowe had been tutor to the Fincham family at Outwell and, disappointed not to have found a position as a schoolmaster, was now chaplain and librarian to the North family. When the vacancy at Castle Acre came up he was encouraged to apply for it by his close friend and celebrated eighteenth-century scholar the Rev. William Stukeley. Chiefly remembered today for 'discovering' Stonehenge and the Druids, Stukeley introduced the concept of pre-history; previously it had been believed that nothing much had been going on in England before the Romans arrived and that they were responsible for all surviving monuments. William Stukeley and Ambrose Pimlowe had been schoolfellows in their native town of Holbeach in Lincolnshire and then members of the Spalding Gentleman's Society, where all manner of topics were discussed from electricity to the rights and wrongs of slavery, much the same subjects as were dissected at the Royal Society in London, of which Stukeley would later be president. So enthusiastic was the twenty-two year old Stukeley for his friend to succeed at Castle Acre that he took it upon himself to call on the four Guardians of Thomas Coke at their London houses and plead his case.

He wrote an amusing letter to Pimlowe in early 1710 describing the difficulties of finding any of the Guardians at home and, if he did, of how they kept him waiting; of going from one end of town to another and back again, and –as so often is the case when several people are to agree upon one matter– the 'maze' he had to wade through with the lawyers, none of whom agreed with each other as to the correct procedure. Should it be a two shilling stamp on the form or a four shilling one? Should all the Trustees (Guardians) have their names on the document or should it be only Mr Coke's? Stukeley's persuasive charms eventually won through.

Pimlowe had had a rival in the guise of the Rev. Mr George, already vicar of West Lexham and son-in-law to Mr Rogers, the Holkham under-bailiff resident in that parish. George had stepped in the minute Briggs died and held services at Castle Acre for the following six months, obliging Pimlowe to wait in the wings.

As chaplain to Mr North, whom he rightly much admired, Pimlowe never actually lived in Castle Acre, for part of his duty was to preside over the household when North was away and to keep him in touch with all local news. A letter he wrote describing 'a little of Norfolk Extravagancies in your Absence may be allowed to interfere with your more innocent Pleasures in Town' contained an account of the Lynn Mart Assembly in February 1718 and the gossip it gave rise to.

North judged Pimlowe to be a most estimable young man of a very high tone and amiability of character; in Stukeley's words Pimlowe was 'a good Scholar, an excellent divine and one of great honesty and simplicity of manners.' Writing after Pimlowe's death in 1750 Stukeley added his sole fault was he smoked too much! Jessop in the nineteenth century believed Pimlowe was a man of scholarly taste and much looked up to in the neighbourhood.

Thus armed with a new tithe book Pimlowe entered the parish of Castle Acre in late summer 1710. Over the next forty years Pimlowe did occasionally have a curate, but on the whole Castle Acre was not only without a resident squire but also a resident vicar.

In an age when most vicars entered the names of their parishioners in English Pimlowe continued to record his in Latin, a pity as he was much given to asides. He managed the odd brief description in that language, for example '*vidua pauper*' (a poor widow) but after 1733, when the law demanded all entries in the registers must be in English, he became more eloquent, describing Thomas Hunsley as: 'A blind beggar but one that can see to get Money and Build a House by his Trade and by his fiddle.'

In 1723 Pimlowe left Rougham to become Rector of Great Dunham, very probably for financial reasons. For most of his adult life Pimlowe supported his unmarried sister Frances who lived with him, and a niece Mary, the daughter of his late brother John, and lent money to several other relatives. Very probably North, who lived on for another twelve years, encouraged Pimlowe to make this move. Great Dunham had forty-four acres of glebe land which Pimlowe was able to let out for £17 a year, whereas in Rougham there was none. At this date Castle Acre still had thirty acres which Pimlowe let to Mr Anderson at the Abbey Farm, together with the vicarage house and the grazing in the churchyard. The vicarage house had needed extensive repairs; it had not been lived in for many years and in 1710 the roof was 'open to the skies'; Pimlowe also had to pay out to fence the churchyard. Despite these extras his income was meagre: when his one maid servant left to get married in 1742 she was not replaced.

His parish clerk was supposed to collect the tithes in the village but from the very beginning in Castle Acre Pimlowe had great difficulties in establishing what the tithes should be and in the reliability of the various people he hoped would prove to be honest when appointed clerk. Dealing with tithes must have been every vicar's least favourite task. It was Stukeley who wrote that the historical proof of the right of clergy to certain tithes amounted to antiquarian research; so that a newly arrived vicar should begin by consulting those in the parish who had lived there the longest and, by these means, discover what the amounts should be. Finding this unsatisfactory, Pimlowe applied to Mr North for legal advice and then set out: 'A True Account of the Profits and Tithes due and payable to the Vicar of Castle Acre'; even then, no amount of 'warm words at the New Inn' (the Ostrich) seems to have resulted in agreement. Despite his best efforts, the feeling that he was being duped never entirely left Pimlowe: he was in constant negotiations over the price of wool and meat with the larger farmers. It was not entirely for himself, for in lean times he showed a generous side towards the poor and excused them their winter dues.

An Act of Parliament of 1722 authorised the purchase of a Poor's House in the village and at this time, before the advent of workhouses, the very poor or infirm of Castle Acre who had no relations to support them lived in 'One Cottage or Town House repaired by the Overseers.' When Ann Hammond, a widow, was buried in 1743 Pimlowe says she came from the Toll House, half way up Bailey Street behind the Old Red Lion and marked on the map of 1779 as a house owned freehold by the parish officers. These officers or Overseers were to find work for the inmates if practical or, if not, they were supported from the taxes imposed on every inhabitant of the parish together with some tithes or charity. The Toll House was small and could house no more than five; later a pair of houses was built on the waste at the edge of Broadmeadow Common.

In Pimlowe's day the interior of Castle Acre church was very plain, with pamments on the floor and the walls limewashed. What would he recognise in the church today? The pulpit, the remains of the rood screens and the font, but little else. There was no heating and the second Sunday service was in the afternoon, to make use of daylight and save on candles. The services were also plain, there may have been some singing but there was no musical accompaniment. It was not until 1793 that a pitch pipe was purchased to sound a note for chanting psalms. By the early eighteenth century most churches had some pews paid for by the more wealthy inhabitants; the remainder of the congregation sat on benches behind or stood. Following the reformation, in the more popular London churches it had become the fashion to pay the churchwardens for a regular seat and where London led, the country followed. Seats in Castle Acre church went with properties: the principal farmers, who were usually the Churchwardens and Overseers, had the seats or pews at the front. The church bells date from Pimlowe's arrival, 1710, and by 1723 there was a clock 'in the steeple.'

The charges made for baptisms, marriages, churchings, burials, and affidavits were a further source of the vicar's income. Regardless of what religion the person was, if you were not registered with the church you could not expect to receive any benefits in time of hardship. It was therefore to your advantage at least to register the birth of your children. In theory the charges were under Pimlowe's control, though they had been agreed to by the churchwardens; for a baptism and churching you might expect to pay 11 pence, publishing banns one shilling and a marriage fee five shillings. In 1710 when Thomas Draper, Mr Blanch's shepherd, married Mr Blanch's maid servant, Pimlowe thought he should charge more, but being new to the parish let it go. However, two years later he felt bold enough to record: 'they' say five shillings 'but I took 6/8'. Burial in the churchyard cost 11 pence if you lived in the village, but five shillings if you came from another parish. Burials in the church itself were considerably more. At Easter each communicant (and again it was in your interest to be one) 'offered' two pence to the church. Pimlowe also received £14 a year from Holkham, in total about £50 a year, from which must be deducted his expenses and the ten per cent of his income he gave to charity.

A lighter moment in the daily round came about in 1713 when the Treaty of Utrecht was signed, ending the Spanish Wars of Succession and bringing peace to England, an event which was celebrated nationally, not least in Castle Acre. The festivities were paid for by the more well-off inhabitants but enjoyed by all. Pimlowe recorded: 'A true account what money was given to be distributed among the poor in Cakes and Ale upon the 7th July 1713 being the Thanksgiving for the Peace happily conducted by Queen Anne ... Mem: the Vicar read Prayers and Preached and Joy Sat in every Countenance and all the way from the Green to the Church Gate were all one Green Bower.' Pimlowe contributed five shillings out of his own pocket; in all £2.15s was collected, more than enough for a very jolly time.

When Pimlowe died in 1749 he was succeeded by the Rev. Thom who stayed only a short while before moving to Southacre. John Coe a stepson of Mr Anderson of Abbey Farm was vicar here sometime and then went to Holkham where he was chaplain to the Cokes until 1775. The next vicar in Castle Acre who remained any length of time was the Rev. Lancaster Framingham; he too had a plurality of parishes and it is unclear how long he actually lived in the village prior to 1783. He died in 1800 and is buried in the church along with his young son and wife.

6 New houses, Newspapers, Art and Culture

SOME NEW houses were built, or re-built in the eighteenth century, along the south side of Stocks Green, where no house had stood for many a year. It was thought that absence of houses on that side of the green was to do with fortifications dating back to the days of the castle and its outer defences, but this is not necessarily so. When building the school in the nineteenth century a well was found dating from the seventeenth century if not earlier. However, it was now that the end house by the churchyard gate (currently Church Gate Tea Rooms) was built 'on the wast' by John Money, the tenant farmer at the Wicken Farm. 'Wast' was land that appeared to be without an owner, though this was not always the opinion of the Lord of the Manor, in this case Thomas Coke of Holkham. Often it was land bordering on or including common land and around the edges of a village green. When Cuckstool Common was built on in 1802, it was entered in the Court Rolls as 'wast' land, being no longer needed as a path to the Mill-in-the-Hole. Another larger piece, too damp to build on and too boggy to farm, has survived by the bridge on the Newton Road.

John Money was tenant at the Wicken from 1734 to his death in 1759, and prosperous enough in 1755 to have bought some freehold land immediately behind the site (being freehold there is no record of this purchase) and now he constructed a house and brewhouse only to find himself in trouble at the next court for 'encroaching on the Lord's wast .... do amerce him one shilling by the year until the said Building shall be removed.' Planning permission had not been granted, but then, as now, it was rare that buildings were actually demolished and by the following court all is regularised. The house remained standing.

SYD DAVISON

Church Gate Tea Rooms, the house buiilt on the wast without permission by John Money, the tenant at The Wicken.

Money was a typical tenant farmer of his time insomuch as he built and owned a house in the village, even if he never lived in it. A build-to-let policy was in vogue; the building to the east of the Ostrich, currently Barnfields, was built as a residential house by an eighteenth century tenant of the Abbey Farm, as was the next building to the east by Charles Boutell, tenant at the Wicken (now the Albert Victor pub). Both were freehold properties. Some marked their houses with their initials on an end gable: large iron letters were a popular method of staking your claim, though many have fallen off in recent years. On his house John Money's initials and the date in the brickwork is still visible from the churchyard. JP can be seen on a cottage near Newton Mill, standing for Joseph Priest miller, and across the river AF on a

44

one-storey cottage stands for Andrew Fountaine of Narford, who owned the parish of Newton. In this case the initials were a marker of where his land began.

Towards the end of the eighteenth century, throughout which parcels of agricultural land were continually being acquired by Holkham, 'new' farmsteads were created. The Lodge Farm was built to the north-east of the village and the Wicken moved to its present position; at the same time some acreage was taken from the Abbey Farm to be added to the Wicken. The concept of a farm house standing in the midst of its own land rather than in the village was a revolutionary one. Cottages for farm workers were built close by with new improved farm buildings for them to work in. At the Priory/Abbey the old tithe barn was pulled down in the mid-nineteenth century, and what was left of a second equally large one belonging to Foxes Manor at the site of the old farm house near the Stone Barn, which had more or less been demolished many years earlier in the great gale of 1713. In the eighteenth century the Stone Barn, which dates from circa 1710, was thatched like most buildings. Opposite, Blanches/the White House farm, now Lower House, was faced with white Holkham brick in 1822 and remained the farmhouse for the middle farm until 1857 when the Manor farm house was built for Thomas Moore Hudson. Manor Farm, along the Westacre road, is nearer to the village centre than either the Lodge or the Wicken.

To return briefly to the eighteenth century, the population of the village grew from circa 540 in 1700 to 842 in 1801, the year of the first census. The ratio of those involved in agricultural labour to those in trade was about two to one. Most families of child-bearing age had children every two years, of whom a large percentage died before the age of twenty. Many women continued to have children well into their forties, often themselves dying shortly afterwards. Instances of illegitimacy were low in the early years of the eighteenth century; many children were conceived before marriage, but in an average of eleven baptisms a year in Pimlowe's time just one born out of wedlock is recorded between 1700 and 1729. If he had refused to baptise any he would have surely recorded the fact, not able to resist an aside. A few were born to men 'defuncti' or 'extinct' but only Deborah Harvey bore a 'filia spuria'. By the 1780s illegitimacy had increased to two or three a year; sometimes the father was known and his name entered. By the nineteenth century the rate was to become higher still.

The eighteenth century saw the widespread introduction of newspapers, and while many people would have been unable to read them, they were often read aloud. Pimlowe had brought a fellow country-man —Marmaduke Summerscales— to Castle Acre, to be clerk and schoolmaster. Summerscales had a spectacularly miserable time in the village even though he received some financial encouragement from Holkham to educate the poor. He was so hard up at one point that Pimlowe bought him new shirts and he set out to seek his fortune elsewhere, but soon returned and shortly afterwards married the twice-widowed Mrs Whisker, moving into her newly built cottage adjoining the Bailey Gate west. He was succeeded by John Hill, schoolmaster for fifty years from 1766-1816.

The status of literacy at this time is unclear. Spreading news such as the loss of a horse —the most common crime, to be compared with car theft— had traditionally been done by 'crying', that is paying the town or village crier to let everyone within the vicinity know who had lost what.

In 1722 the *Norwich Mercury* was founded. Relying at first on reprinting stories from the London papers, it came out weekly on Saturdays and while it took people a while to see how newspapers

SYD DAVISON

The east end of Lower House on St. James's Green, previously the White House Farm, showing a nineteenth-century extension to the south

could be used locally, by the 1740s the power of advertising had been understood. In 1746 Castle Acre took space in the paper to announce its Sheep Fair, to be held on July 25. It was expensive to advertise but rewarding and adverts for the Fair became an annual investment. By the 1750s the newspaper was regularly on sale in Swaffham at Mr Fortin's and at Fakenham at Mr Stocking's. At both these places advertisements could be placed. Between 1746 and 1775 Castle Acre appeared sixty-five times in the *Norwich Mercury*; in April 1759 an unnamed house was offered for sale, in December of the same year 'a Publick House known by the sign of the Green Man ... completely finished with set of brewing utensils, a convenient yard and stable worth £10 in rent.' This property is in Bailey Street, later known as

The Ship, on the corner of Pales Green. In 1774 the widow of a village butcher Mary Barker 'returns her most grateful thanks to the customers of her late husband' and asks them to settle their accounts. Anyone who has any demand on her husband's estate is to direct their business to Mr Stanford of Little Massingham or Mr John Burgess of Castle Acre, the executors. Mr Burgess was a farmer. This is immediately followed by a second announcement placed by Samuel Brooks, late Journeyman to Mary Barker's husband, who is taking on the business and 'humbly requests the Continuance of the Favors of the Customers'. This type of announcement is unusual for a village business, both costly and elaborate, more likely to be found in a town, and suggests that at this date enough people in the village and surrounding area would be able to read it and appreciate the service they were offered.

Looking north up Drury Lane, the barn used as a theatre was at the far end of the house on the left.

Castle Acre can claim a link with Admiral Horatio Nelson, whose father had been vicar of Sporle across the valley. The Nelson family were far more local to this area than to Burnham Thorpe where the Admiral was born and which is usually associated with him. Successive generations of Nelsons had owned land in Castle Acre from at least the sixteenth to the mid-eighteenth centuries and are his direct ancestors. They owned several houses in the village, one of which can be seen immediately south of the Bailey Gate on the east side and contains a greater than usual amount of stone in its walls. At the Swaffham celebrations for the victory of the Nile in 1797, Nelson was indeed seen as a local hero and a pub on the Castle Acre road was so named.

To compete with Swaffham and other towns Castle Acre had its share of culture, a 'theatre', and Muckleborrow Lane was renamed Drury Lane in its honour, a slightly ironic change. The theatre was in fact a barn visited from time to time by strolling players. The one surviving bill for 1812 shows it was not the well known Fisher company that came here but the Eldreds. In the week preceding Christmas of that year they offered a performance of *The Soldier's Daughter* followed by the farce *Animal Magnetism* – as was the fashion – on the Tuesday, and *She Stoops to Conquer* and *Ghost* on the Thursday. The doors opened at half past five and the play began an hour later. The Manager assured the Ladies and Gentlemen of Castle Acre that he had spared no expense in rendering the theatre warm and comfortable, having a fireplace in the front of the boxes. The choice of boxes 3/-, the pit 2/- or the gallery 1/- was the same as in any other theatre. Children under ten were allowed in at half price and some of the seats were offered at reduced rates, doubtless those where the view was obscured by a timber post. It is probable that, though the name Drury stuck to the lane, the barn did not house the theatre for many more seasons.

A hundred years later in 1930 an investigating journalist interviewed the oldest inhabitants but could find no one with any memories of it; most were unaware it had ever existed.

Mrs Anne Framingham, widow of the vicar and with no surviving children, had been living in rented accommodation in Castle Acre for about thirty-five years at the time of her death in 1818. Her will allows us another view into the cultural life of the village. In it she lists her silverware, candlesticks, sugar scoop, the 'little ornaments on my chimney piece … a square mahogany card table, copper tea kettle and coffee mill.' Her two beneficiaries were her 'dear affectionate well beloved friend' Ann Larpent of Sloane Street, Chelsea and Ann Barton, whose father was the tenant at Lodge Farm.

Ann Larpent was sister to Mr John Larpent the inspector of plays, a civil servant who worked for the Lord Chamberlain and without whose approval no play was given a licence to perform. His wife Ann Margaretta Larpent, a cultured and intellectual woman, is chiefly known today for her diary; in her time she personified self-improvement by way of literature, the arts and learning.

This glimpse into gentility is not to suggest that Castle Acre in any way resembled a Cranford at this date, it did not, despite a period when women held positions of some influence in the village. Catherine Balls was landlady at the Ostrich Inn from 1758 to 1780; at Foxes immediately prior to the building of the Lodge Farm, Widow Abell was tenant from 1770-1791 and at the Wicken the tenants were two sisters named Boutell 1779-1793. Sabra Griggs, born in Castle Acre in 1760, was in a position to buy a piece of the 'wast' ground at Cuckstool Lane in 1802 and here she built a pair of one-storey cottages, possibly for herself and her sister Charlotte. Their initials can still be seen on the gable end of what has since become a house.

Two years later at the age of forty-four Sabra married Henry Flood of Great Dunham and moved there. After the death of her sister Sabra left the cottages to her great-nephew and they were eventually sold to Holkham in 1917 when a first floor storey was added. The lower one built for Sabra is of flint and the upper of brick, with Holkham making its mark by installing a fireplace with their Ostrich emblem in an upstairs bedroom. What influence these independent women had, directly or indirectly, on village life can only be imagined. But were there tourists to what we now consider is a picturesque village, at least by Norfolk standards? Nathaniel Buck had drawn the Priory and the

Cotman's drawing of the Priory; the seventeenth-century infill can be seen on the extreme right. It was demolished in 1929 when the Priory was given into the care of the Office of Works, now English Heritage

Castle for Thomas Coke in 1738 and these were printed and would have had a wide circulation. In 1728 Matthew Dekker staying with Sir Andrew Fountaine at Narford had glanced in the direction of the Priory ruins and in 1777 Hannah More wrote a description of them. In 1804 young John Sell Cotman spent a week here, staying at the Ostrich Inn now run by Thomas Boyce one time coachman to Thomas William Coke, where by day he sketched in and around the Castle and the Priory. Swaffham had long been fashionable for racing and its accompanying assemblies, with concerts by Dr Burney of Lynn attended by the great and the good, and London hairdressers on hand to help the local ladies with the latest fashions. Though for most of the eighteenth century it was more usual to visit houses than ancient sites that nobody seemed to know much about, nevertheless Castle Acre must have been a tempting venue for a picnic. By the nineteenth century the age of romantics and the vogue for ruins had well and truly begun.

7 Declining Fortunes – the aftermath of War

HOWEVER, THE vast majority of village inhabitants (and the population was rising steadily) were poor, and when Mrs Framingham died in 1818, at the end of the wars with France, life for most of them was about to become worse. In 1821, when asked to let a Holkham-owned cottage to a labourer from Westacre, Coke wrote he agreed but only for a year: 'however inconvenient to my Tenantry, the want of cottages for those who belong to this parish [Castle Acre] is become a very serious evil, and the building of new ones is attended with a very heavy expense, particularly in these times'. Henry Abbott, tenant at the Wicken, took a more optimistic view; he recorded in the same year that, with the exception of one or two old people, every labourer in the village was in employment. This was not to last: inflation followed conflict, poor harvests in the 1820s, increased taxes and harsh corn laws generated economic gloom. Home industry such as spinning or weaving had largely disappeared as uneconomic for those who distributed and collected the work, and finding employment as a day labourer was becoming harder as farmers cut back and the competition grew more fierce. Even the farmers suffered; Mr Dewing, who had married one of the Miss Boutells in 1792 and thus inherited the tenancy at the Wicken, despite new premises having been built for him and a new farm house, was failing badly by 1816. He was too ill, so he said, to attend the Audit at Holkham and in arrears with the rent. It went from bad to worse; by 1820 the expensive new farmhouse was in need of extensive repairs, 'contrary to every Holkham principle' and a notice to quit was served. The Dewings hung on for another year but, unable to find enough to pay what they owed, were obliged to sell 'every bed, table, chair and spoon' to meet the creditors.

Thomas William Coke the landlord moved them into part of Weasenham Hall where they were to live rent free and gave them a pension of £2 a week. But Dewing, 'a respectable old person' of fifty-four, died within a month, and his widow seven years later. The great prosperity that the Boutells had enjoyed in earlier times (and the Dewings, previously tenants at Westacre) was now quite gone.

They were not alone: at the Lodge Farm young Mr Turner, who had insisted that marble fireplaces should be installed both upstairs and down among other extravagances when he arrived in 1816, was behindhand with the rent within a year and unable to catch up; he was obliged to quit just six years later. Blanches, the third farm in the village, was also in trouble. Thomas Purdy had taken it in 1809; he had previously been a Holkham tenant at Egmere and Weasenham and was the winner of several cups for breeding South Down and Leicester sheep, but even he could not make a go of things. Like the others he was in arrears by 1817 and quit in January 1822, owing Coke not only the rent but a personal debt of £2,308. It is believed that both he and Turner left bankrupt. This farm and the Lodge were sub-sequently let to John Hudson senior and junior at reduced rents. Despite the hardness of the times there were still many whose great-est ambition was to be a Holkham tenant. Henry Abbott, who succeeded the Dewings at the Wicken, had written the most flowery letters to Coke, pleading to be allowed a lease. Both the Hudsons and Abbott must have been fully aware of the challenges ahead.

Meanwhile the property-owning villagers observed the comings and goings with interest; these were people who owned their houses freehold along with their gardens and small parcels of land, which they now viewed as potential building plots. As the population grew the lack of accommodation, noted by Holkham but not acted upon, encouraged the far-sighted among them to exploit the situation to

SYD DAVISON

Mr High's house in the High Street

their own gain. The most prolific of these entrepreneurs was John Harvey; along with others he began to build, infilling small shanty cottages where once there were yards and gardens. Bricks were easily obtainable; they were made in the village by Isaac Comer and to bind them there were lime kilns on hand. The present house near the Grove opposite the old butcher's shop in the High Street is seen to have a sort of moat in front of it; this was nothing to do with the castle, Mr High who lived there had a lime pit. As farmers tightened their belts, agricultural labourers were laid off in other parishes, turned out of their tied cottages and made homeless; Castle Acre speculators were ready and able to offer them accommodation.

Castle Acre was never a purely agricultural village; formerly a market town, it was still a centre for shopping and services for the surrounding region. In 1845 it had, for instance, corn mills, a brickworks, saddlers, a limekiln, a tannery, a maltings, two smithies, wheel-wrights, joiners, saddlers, bakers, shoemakers, several shops, (grocers, drapers, butchers, a chemist) five public houses plus three beer houses. It would seem to offer varied employment to labourers and some domestic service for their womenfolk, for example at the vic-arage and the doctor's house. But most of these businesses were small family affairs and wages were low; craftsmen took on apprentices, not farm labourers. On top of which, whereas at one time labourers were employed through the winter threshing corn by flail, by 1840 most farmers had threshing machines.

Even so both single men and families flocked to the village, grate-ful for what they could find, but they were often suspected of being troublemakers and poachers, though there is no real evidence to prove this; nevertheless Castle Acre came to be known as 'the coop of all the scrapings in the county.' John Harvey owned over thirty cottages in the village all let at an average and exorbitant rent of £4.10s a year, more than double that charged by Holkham. To meet these rents, which date from the 1830s, a solution was found that did not involve the men: redundant for the most part, they looked on while their women and children went out in gangs on the land weeding and hoeing. It was a desperate solution for many families.

John Hudson, the farmer at Lodge Farm who arrived in Castle Acre in 1822, stated that the gang system was unknown at that date, though men had been hired out or loaned in groups for agricultural labour since earliest times. The Castle Acre gangs were to become notorious for mainly employing women and children, their nimble fingers suit-able for weeding and their pay far less than men's. Women earned 8d a day, unmarried girls 6d and children 4d.

To help over their lean times many farmers had reductions made in their rents, and now both Hudson and his father (the latter at the newly named White House Farm on account of its having been faced with the best white Holkham bricks), along with Stephen Abbott (Henry's son) at the Wicken, engaged with two Castle Acre gangmasters Fuller and Moulton to have their fields cleared of stones, weeded and their turnips gathered by women and children. The working hours were from dawn to dusk with no meal break. All too often the overseers employed by the gangmasters were harsh and the children whipped if they did not work hard enough, at home their diet was poor – bread, potatoes and dumplings. They would have fared better in the workhouse or prison.

There was, however, always plenty of work: with so many neighbouring farms turning off their labourers and consequently being short of workers the gangs were in demand outside the parish, involving walks of up to ten miles. When the weather was bad they received no pay. It was estimated that Fuller had about a hundred women and children working for him and it did not stop there: he owned cottages in the village where his workers lived and forced them to buy their groceries (flour) from his shop and no other. Castle Acre gangs, made up of women and children, worked on farms in Southacre, Newton, Narford, Westacre, Walton, Gayton Thorpe, Rougham, Weasenham, Lexham and Sporle.

The gangmasters did very nicely and those that employed them seemed largely unconcerned at the conditions of work. For the most part people ignored the plight of the lowly gang workers. Hudson of Lodge Farm, who had won a number of agricultural prizes by 1843 and was a founder member of the newish (1838) Royal Agricultural Society, believed in the gang system, though he said that Castle Acre was a thoroughly depraved place. Hammond, the main landowner at Westacre, agreed with him. He believed that, properly supervised, there was little danger of the gang workers stealing from their employers.

The gang system allowed the female workers 'opportunities', and this was blamed for the increase in illegitimate births, which rose to a record twenty-two in 1838, further fuelling the prejudices. The vicar of South Acre, showing a breathtaking lack of insight, felt the question of morals was something that should be tackled in the home; he even suggested that with proper supervision the gang system could be used as a means of 'improving the moral tone of the people'. As a direct result of their work in the fields these women were regarded as no longer fitted for domestic service and were at greater risk of being seduced than others ... their dress was considered provocative, skirts hoisted up, and much violence and petty crime was blamed on them. A very high rate of infant mortality existed among the babies of women who worked in gangs; locally it is said this was often due to poppy seeds crushed and fed to them to keep them docile while their mothers were at work. Hudson retorted helpfully 'if you want to judge by illegitimate births, look into your own kitchens.'

By way of compensation the girls developed a camaraderie of their own. Several observers said they were unnerved by the bold looks and manners of gang girls returning from work, while a former curate, the Rev. R. Jackson stated 'I have been to Sierre Leone, but I have seen shameless wickedness in Castle Acre such as I never witnessed in Africa. I have sometimes, when taking my walks, had the misfortune to have a gang of twelve or twenty young women following at my heels, and the obscenity of their conversation and the lewdness of the songs they sang were such as needed to be heard to be believed.' Would that he had written them down.

The gang system began to attract unfavourable comment, though from whom it is unclear, resulting in a Poor Law Commission for the counties of Suffolk, Norfolk and Lincoln undertaken by Mr Stephen Charles Denison in 1843. His report on Castle Acre was extremely thorough; he took evidence from employers, employees and gang-masters, and estimated that over a hundred families were living in extreme misery. The facts he collected were shocking; the exploitation of the workers by gangmasters and their overseers, children of six years old having to walk from five to seven miles to their work and then if it rained, to walk back again without earning anything, and the seeming indifference of the landowners and farmers, led him to conclude that Castle Acre was the most wretched rural parish he had ever seen. All the same he conceded that to end the gang system would only be the cause of even greater poverty 'and the immorality and crime of the place would be increased by idleness and distress'.

So what happened as a result of this report? Not a lot. Samuel Pegler, a Superintendent of Police, was resident in the village by 1845, and was succeeded in rapid succession by Thomas Smith in 1847, PC Richard Proctor in 1849 and Richard Banker from Sussex in 1851. It was not until twenty-four years later in 1867 that an Act of Parliament designed to regulate gangs was passed. The improvement was hardly more than moderate: no children under eight to do farm work, women gangmasters where females were employed and the gangmasters to be licensed by JPs. By then, some conceded, times were a little better. That same year, 1867, a woman, Hannah Bloye, employed in a gang on Hudson's farm said he was a good master and paid towards her daughter's schooling.

In 1851 Holkham commissioned its own report on those parts of Castle Acre in its ownership. The Lodge Farm is described as 'an exceedingly fine occupation ... managed with the greatest skills and liberality.' The Wicken is equally glowingly depicted, the White House, renamed Lower Farm, and the much reduced Abbey Farm pass with fewer positive adjectives. The house at the Abbey was considered 'old, small and not well arranged … the roof is defective and admits the rain in several places. There are two comfortable sitting rooms and six or seven small bedrooms'. Newton Mill is said to be out of repair, 'not a desirable occupation having very little or no business' while the few acres surrounding it 'evidently receive very little attention.'

Of the thirty-one Holkham cottages in the parish they varied from being well built with two bedrooms for three people, to Churchman's cottage where *seven* people shared the one bedroom. Not surprisingly the Churchman family feature as an example of the depraved inhabitants that gave the village its bad name. A Churchman daughter, Maria, possibly born in Gayton Workhouse, was described as a 'most notorious and determined Virago' when she was charged with being drunk and disorderly; she was to have at least one illegitimate child born in the workhouse in 1866.

Castle Acre had become a microcosm of all the ills that come from poverty and overcrowding, though in a rural setting. If ever there was an example of the effects of desperate vulnerability and exploitation then this is it.

By the mid-nineteenth century the population had grown to 1,567, an increase of 74% since 1811, a far faster rate than most other parishes and the village was bursting at the seams. The census of 1851 shows that forty-seven of the 334 households were headed by male incomers who had married Castle Acre wives and of the village 'businesses' more than half were managed by people born elsewhere, though they may have had familial connections to account for this. Family life was hard to sustain as a consequence of the gangs; fathers felt their wives and children were undercutting them; parents might wish their children to be educated but could neither afford the penny a week fees nor do without the children's earnings. The gang system endured, though it is salutary to see how many men in the 1851 census are entered as Agricultural Labourers and how few women as Field Workers or a variant, yet we know from other sources that women and children continued to make up the majority of the gangs long after this date. For many women field work was regarded as impermanent, though in fact it was not so.

The fate of the gangmaster James Moulton is unknown, but he may, like James Fuller, have experienced a road to Damascus conversion and become a Methodist and a Ranter. Fuller was always an extremist, he did nothing by halves and after his conversion built a Ranters Chapel in Pales Green; it is on the east side and can easily be recognised by the arched windows. Ranters were Primitive Methodists and unlike Wesleyan Methodists they were politically active. Part of his accumulated riches went towards the re-building of the Swaffham Methodist chapel in London Street, where he laid a foundation stone on September 10 1873. Thanks to a careless manager this stone was covered in cement and lost to posterity when, in 1998, a lavatory was built at the side of the chapel.

A bonus for the village children was the creation of Sunday Schools: these existed primarily to teach reading so that children could study the Bible but they also provided them with a meal. The schools were free, and the children were able to attend as they did not work on Sundays. In the 1840s there were three in Castle Acre: Church of England, Methodist and Baptist, with over two hundred children on their books.

Not surprisingly Nonconformists flourished in the village; Castle Acre had been on the Swaffham Circuit of Wesleyan Methodists since 1813 and in 1830 had a small Wesleyan Chapel built on the Newton Road but, from the first, Wesleyans appealed mainly to shopkeepers and artisans, and did not attract the bulk of those drawn to non-

HELEN BREACH

The Village Hall on the castle ditches, previously the Baptist Chapel

conformity. By 1836 Baptists were established in the village and shortly afterwards Mr High, the builder and lime-kiln owner, sold them part of his orchard on the steep bank of the castle's ditches, where they built a chapel. The first soon proved too small and was extended to more than three times its original size; it is now the Village Hall. The bath used for baptisms can still be found under the stage at the eastern end of the building.

Primitive Methodists, who appealed more to the agricultural labourers than the Wesleyans, arrived in Swaffham in 1825 but it was not until 1878 that they built a chapel and schoolroom in Bailey Street. John Might, aged twenty-eight from Sculthorpe, was the Methodist Minister in 1851 and Jabez Stutterd, aged thirty from Colne in Lancashire, the Baptist.

The advent of non-conformity in the village had been noted with some alarm by the Church of England well before 1830, not least because the vicar, the Rev. Tickell, resided twenty-five miles away at Wells-next-the-Sea, leaving his duties to a less than an satisfactory curate William Gibbs. A letter in the Holkham archives from the Bishop of Norwich dated July 3, 1830 refers to many conversations the Bishop had had with Thomas William Coke on the subject of Castle Acre and, while not mentioning the Wesleyans and Baptists by name, he wrote that the parish '... in a religious point of view is most deplorable, a very numerous population, a Curate of very indifferent Character ...' Among his list of Gibbs's failings the Bishop records he held only one service on a Sunday while previously there had been two 'and neglects the numerous other duties of an attentive Pastor.' Bishop Stanley was a reforming Bishop and took these matters seriously, with some justification. One June morning just three years previously a letter arrived at Holkham describing the scene at the Ostrich Inn on Sunday May 20. Abbott, the Wicken tenant (also one of the Churchwardens and Overseers), reported that the landlord Rumbelow had 'his House full of company at the time of Divine Service, with much drunkenness, riot and confusion ... I remonstrated with him on the impropriety of such practice, I did not think him altogether civil.' It was by no means the first time this had happened and Abbott threatened to prevent the renewal of Rumbelow's licence. Rumbelow was the son-in-law of the previous landlord of the Ostrich, Thomas Boyce, who in turn had been Coke's coachman. He was ordered by Holkham to 'solicit the forgiveness of Mr Abbott ... and promise never to offend in like manner again'. This he must have done, for he remained landlord for another seven years. Tickell was in part responsible, for after disputing the Vicarial tithes due to him –much as Pimlowe had done a hundred years previously– he seldom, if ever, visited the village again. Tickell was also Rector of Wighton but preferred Wells to both places. In 1816, backed by a paid legal advisor, he had held a meeting at the Ostrich to claim increased tithes in Castle Acre, but lost his case. His curate Gibbs had been in the village since at least 1815. Following the Bishop's recommendation, Gibbs's responsibilities were lessened. Rather than 'reduce him to absolute beggary' the Bishop kindly allowed him the curacies of Newton and Lexham, where less harm could be done 'the number being committed to his care being small and consequently his example less extensively dangerous'. On the tithe map of 1838 Gibbs was living on the outskirts of Castle Acre close to Newton Mill. In his place came the Rev. Robert Jackson, a more energising curate who, within months of his appointment, set up the Church of England Sunday School in early 1831 and soon claimed to have an attendance of over a hundred children. This number was too great to squeeze into the school room at the back of the church: the overflow, sanctioned by Holkham, set up in the chancel huddled round a stove.

No more is heard of 'riotous' Sunday morning drinking sessions at the Ostrich; nevertheless Castle Acre's reputation for an interesting mixture of free-thinkers and debauched morals was one that lasted well into the second half of the twentieth century; by then people rather enjoyed it.

8 Education and re-thinking the Priory

IN 1813, the same year that Castle Acre joined the Swaffham circuit of Wesleyan Methodists, a Church of England School affiliated to the National Society was opened in the village. National Schools were financed by subscriptions and donations from local people, school pence from the pupils and grants from the National Society, itself financed by subscribers. Attendance was not compulsory and there are no surviving records of this establishment. There had been some form of education in the village since at least the time of Ambrose Pimlowe who paid Mrs Elizabeth Smith from his own pocket to teach 'four poor Children', she taught in conjunction with Marmaduke Summerscales until circa 1735. A Mrs Helen Beales was paid to teach in the 1730s with a Mr Davey, until 1739 when Isaac Tolhe was the schoolmaster. The burial register records James Large was school-master until 1768 and then John Hill, who died in 1816 aged 80, schoolmaster for fifty years. By 1836 there were two academies in the village, one run by Robert Mays and the other by John Pratt.

It was felt by the Rev. Bloom, who had been appointed vicar of Castle Acre in 1836, that the competing Sunday Schools run by the non-conformists posed a threat to the Church of England. Unlike Tickell, Bloom lived in the village throughout his ministry. In 1838 he wrote to Thomas William Coke, lately created earl of Leicester, to suggest that a purpose-built school would be a great asset to the village and informed him of an appropriate site. Bloom had some reason to feel optimistic, as the previous year the earl had paid out towards new school buildings in Great Massingham and North Elmham. His effusive letter when hearing from the Holkham agent that the earl was in agreement is pure Uriah Heap. The site in question opposite the Ostrich Inn was currently a small field under cultivation; it was part of the Ostrich 'farm' and planted with a crop of potatoes. Bloom persuaded his Bishop and others to raise £150 for 'a very neat semi-Gothic building comprising two School Rooms each capable of containing one Hundred Children, the Total Expence ... not to exceed £180.'

The school was duly built and it completed the infilling on the south side of Stocks Green; it was enlarged in 1873 and by then had 349 children on the roll with an average attendance of 270. It was in 1848 that the Rev. Bloom 'by singular chance found in our School Yard ... an ancient and excellent Well, in a perfect state of Repair...no knowledge or Tradition of a Well in this place exists as far as I can ascertain in the Memory of the oldest Inhabitant.' He measured it, a drop of twenty-five feet, but was advised it would be at least sixty. Asking what should be done, the answer came from Holkham to fill it in.

Children entered the school at the age of three and stayed until fourteen; from 1902 onwards a few won scholarships to Grammar Schools. Today the school is a Primary one.

The Rev. Bloom was instrumental in bringing the Priory and Castle to the attention of the young second earl of Leicester who inherited the Holkham estate in 1842. Bloom wrote a book about the village and its heritage, published in 1843 financed by public subscription to which the earl contributed; whether he read it or not we cannot know, but some eleven years later a further re-arrangement of the Castle Acre farms took place. The Abbey Farm ceased to be: its land was taken in to form part of the new Manor farm created for the young Hudson of the third generation, John Moore Hudson. The Manor Farmhouse was built on the Westacre road with a fine view sweeping south down towards the Nar; it was said by members of the family that its fine oak interior doors were made from a wreck washed up on Holkham beach.

Even grander plans were drawn up for the future of the Abbey/Priory when the London architects Dean and Bellhouse were commissioned to restore the Prior's Lodgings in the Gothic style. Possibly the earl had in mind a shooting lodge for himself; Castle Acre had a tradition of being a fine part of the county for partridge. Fortunately only the plans have survived – the work was never carried out; perhaps Bloom reminded him that the Priory ruins were Norman and not Gothic. At all events a gardener from distant Surrey (Clapham, actually) was installed as the new tenant of the Priory and given orders to keep the place tidy. His name was Merritt and he lived and worked at the Priory from 1860 to his death in 1889, his widow Mary succeeding him for another three years. Meanwhile, the earl revised his plans and ordered notice boards for the 'Castle Acre Ruins' and paid for repairs done to the buildings.

Towards the end of the century an archaeologist W. H. St. John Hope of the Society of Antiquaries spent part of several summers working at the Priory and it was he who recommended to the earl, after the death of Merritt, that the site should be fenced and a resident caretaker employed to prevent vandalism, and that visitors be allowed in only on payment of 6d a time. He also suggested a guide book should be produced. After choosing a totally unsuitable man 'who has done *nothing* to keep the place tidy' Robert Addison, the parish clerk, was taken on; he was a conscientious fellow but elderly and lame. Fortunately his son Rufus was a gardener. In 1892 the number of visitors paying 6d a time was 416. Ruins, Norman or otherwise, were popular and Castle Acre was reasonably accessible – the railway brought people to Swaffham, the station was on the Castle Acre road and enterprising locals ran carrier waggons from there to the village. The Ostrich elevated itself to a Hotel.

The Abbey, as it was persistently called, was open over the summer months, twenty-seven weeks a year, but was never a money-making enterprise. In 1899 the cost to Holkham for Custodian's wages and books of tickets came to £10 8s 0d, income from visitors £12 9s 9d, profit £2.1s 9d. Addison was Custodian from 1901 to 1919 the year he died. He was succeeded by a Mrs Goldsmith until 1928 when it was agreed that the Ministry of Works should take over. From 1929 to the 1960s a Castle Acre man, Mr Savage, was Custodian. Like his predecessor Mr Addison he kept the site open all through the war; during the First World War visitors numbers kept up, how many came between 1939 and 1945 is not known.

At Holkham Thomas Banner had been Clerk of the Works from 1859 to some time in the late 1870s when he took semi-retirement and moved to Castle Acre. Banner came from Lancashire and in the census of 1891 he is described as Architect, which he would have needed to be to care for such a house as Holkham. He had had his eye on Castle Acre for some time, and as early as 1864 bought land here and in due course left his mark: a house he built for himself on the Newton Road, Ivy Cottage and a pair of double cottages next door (Oak Cottages). These he built for his two sons John, a carpenter, and Thomas, a stonemason; they appear in Kelly's Directory of 1879 as the Banner Brothers joiners and general and monumental masons. The proximity to their father may have been a little too close, for they did not live there for long, though Banner stayed on in Castle Acre to his death in 1900.

From the early years of the nineteenth century Castle Acre had a resident doctor/surgeon. Later an imposing house was built for him in Bailey Street on the east side: Marcon House, just north of the Old Red Lion; red brick with wrought-iron railings in front and a surgery entrance to one side, an urban design that stood out among the mainly

Robert Addison, the parish clerk taken on as the resident caretaker at the Priory

flint cottages. Another red brick house built about this time, on the site of some old cottages, was Norfolk House on Newton Road, for Augustus Barrett grocer and draper.

These houses were an exception: despite the 1851 report on the state of the cottages in Castle Acre owned by the Holkham estate, between 1850 and 1880 more was spent on church building and restoration than on new cottages. In 1875 the earl paid £2,450 to repair and improve the church; a new floor was put down, the vestry re-roofed, and new gates purchased. The following year a new vicarage was built, also paid for in part by Holkham. The vicarage had six bed-rooms, two dressing rooms, a water closet but no bathroom. No new vicarage had been built since before Pimlowe's day: the Rev. Bloom had rented The Grove.

9 Harsh Times

THE SECOND farming depression of the century in the 1880s saw continuing hardship, though an attempt to alleviate the poverty was the creation of allotments. Prior to the formation of the civil Parish Council in 1894, allotments rents for Castle Acre payable to the Holkham estate amounted to £41 and were administered by the Parochial Church Council; in keeping with tradition, all notices about them were pinned to the church doors. After 1894 the civil District Council arranged for a more formal agreement with the landowners, in this case Holkham and Mr Fountaine at Narford. Those residents of Castle Acre wishing to continue with their allotments, and those who wanted one, were asked to apply in writing. By 1895 seventy-seven acres were needed to accommodate all those who had applied, allowing each applicant a quarter of an acre. The land for the allotments was of course taken from the farms; Mr T. M. Hudson of the Manor Farm was not in favour of this; Mr Everington, who had succeeded old Mr John Hudson at the Lodge Farm, was. Allotment matters dominated the civil Parish Council meetings for many years.

At the same time 'new' rules were passed by the Parish Council to keep the river and drains clear, to control grazing stock on the commons and repeating the time-old notice that it was an offence to take flaggs etc. off the commons without prior permission (last entered in the Court Rolls in the seventeenth century.)

Some indication of how the agricultural labourers and their families lived in the nineteenth century was recorded in an interview published in 1915. The occasion was the birthdays of Mr and Mrs Mobbs who were both due to reach the age of ninety-one, he in June and she in July. They had been married for sixty-seven years (1849) and Mr Mobbs had worked for the same family, the Hudsons, for seventy-three years. The article was entitled 'Hard Times at Castle Acre'; interviewed in 'the spotless state of their cosy sitting room' the journalist learnt how Mr Mobbs had earned eight shillings a week for days that began at five in the morning and ended at eight at night. For his midday meal he had taken with him most days a pudding made from a half penny worth of suet and a bottle of cold water, on others a bit of bread and onion. Mrs Mobbs had also worked on the land, pulling turnips and hoeing wheat, earning 8d a day, out of which she paid for their children to go to school. Mrs Mobbs recounted how she had learnt her letters at Sunday School but could not put them together; when she was fifty she thought she could teach herself to read and had a desire to buy a Bible. Her gangmaster agreed to get her one. 'I could repay him as I was able. He knew he was sure of his money because I was in his gang.'

Mr and Mrs Mobbs had a hero, Joseph Arch, who as they explained brought wages up to ten shillings a week after his visit to the village. 'God bless Joseph Arch I say ! ... he talked to us on the village green and soon afterwards wages went up.' Previously Mr and Mrs Mobbs had been dependent on the parish for bread; even so, the most Mr Mobbs ever earned was twelve shillings a week and that took a lot of managing, many times Sunday dinner was only bread with a turnip or a cabbage. 'Nobody lived harder than we did ... work hard, live plain ... gone into the pantry and looked at the loaf and daren't cut a piece off ... nobody on earth knows what my poor little stomach has felt in the past when I've been at our chapel looking at one and then at another and I've thought: Did they feel like I did ?' Mr and Mrs Mobbs lived long enough to get off the parish and enjoy the benefits of the post 1908 pension. In 1915 they were able to report they were 'Never better off in our lives ... it's the pension you know.'

These hard times resulted in many leaving the village. From letters I have received from people tracing their families it seems that a few went abroad, mainly to Canada, but most went north into the midlands to work in heavy industries, especially mining, a cruel fate for country boys. Others went to London and found more familiar work as grooms, but few returned. In the 1851 census 251 men are described as agricultural labourers, of which 150 were born in Castle Acre, the oldest seventy-six and the youngest nine. In 1891 the number had gone down to 189, of whom 127 were Castle Acre born. At least one of those, even though in employment, was to leave in 1893 taking his wife and children with him to become a Nottinghamshire miner.

So severe was the agricultural depression that Holkham had to advertise in Scottish newspapers in order to find tenants for their farms; whereas the Abbots and their like had fought tooth and nail to get a Holkham lease earlier in the century even in the wake of a severe depression, the situation was now very different. The new tenants who arrived at the Wicken at this time –the Keiths– came all the way from Aberdeen.

Agricultural workers dressed in their Sunday best on Stocks Green at the time of the 1923 strike

Sir George Edwards of the Agricultural Union enjoying a game of bowls at Castle Acre with three Castle Acre residents, all members of the Parish Council: Messrs Gaze, Willgress and Pightling

10 Slow progress: 1900 onwards

THE POPULATION of Castle Acre declined by 1900 to about a thousand, though the list of names on the First World War Memorial is longer than many another village of comparable size. In the Castle Acre census of 1851 five men are described as Chelsea Pensioners, that is soldiers either invalided out of the army or retired after twenty years service. Two of them were old enough to have served in the Napoleonic wars and another two, still in their forties, and according to the births of their youngest children only recently returned to the village, had probably spent time in Ireland, as both had wives born in Limerick. All five had tales of travel and war to recount to those who would listen, whereas forty years on, not one soldier appears in the 1891 census. Does this go some way to explain the innocent enthusiasm with which so many walked to Dereham in 1914 to enlist? Once signed up they were allocated to a variety of different regiments. The first to be killed in action in October 1914 was Reginald Porter, the doctor's son; he was born in Castle Acre and aged twenty-six at the time of his death. Of the others one or two were professional soldiers such as Serjeant Major Askew, old enough to have fought in the Boer War; several were in their late thirties, others still in their teens. Most drew their last breath in France but at least three were killed in Turkey, one in Iraq and two in Palestine.

In the wake of Joseph Arch the last years of the nineteenth century had seen the formation of the first ever agricultural workers union founded by George Edwards, then living in Fakenham; he visited Castle Acre frequently, where photographs show him playing bowls with the elder members of the community.

In the strike of 1923 agricultural labourers, exclusively men, turned out in large numbers in their Sunday best to demonstrate on Stocks Green and police were called in to escort those who had not joined but continued to plough. For an agricultural worker the decision to strike was harder than for most; striking meant neglecting *their* land, for it was they who worked it, not the landlord or even the farmer, and making such a choice did not come easily. They risked not only their jobs but also their accommodation.

The 1920s also saw the vogue for pageants and whimsy, the name Stocks Green for the green in the middle of the village first appears about this time; previously it was Church Green and there is no record that there ever were stocks there, cuckstools at Cuckstool Lane definitely, but stocks less certain. Morris dancing and the like were 'revived' and re-emerged usually greatly changed from the original. Cecil Sharp collected folk songs and in July 1927 a huge pageant over three days was held at the Abbey/Priory. The Marchioness Townshend of Raynham posed as the Virgin Mary in a tableau, in direct imitation of Lady Diana Cooper, while around her massed the clergy, some *bonafide* like the Bishop of Norwich, others dressed up for the day, and hordes of extras representing the races on earth 'Africa, India, China, Egypt, Japan and the Jews'. A pious report in the *Eastern Daily Press* lamented the threatening grey skies.

From 1892 the fishing rights in the river, which had variously been under the control of the monks, the tenant farmers, and the miller at Newton, were let to a group of enthusiasts who formed the Castle Acre Fishing Club. Stories of poachers would fill a chapter. Suffice it to say that during the period of the great sheep-shearings at Holkham in the early nineteenth century many a diner feasted on trout caught in the Nar at Castle Acre. The fishing club, which still exists, was

MR GOODCHILD, PURDY'S

*A scene from the pageant which was held over three days
at the Priory in July 1927.*

small, seldom more than eight members, most of whom did not live
in the village.

As early as 1911 the poor state of the houses built by the speculators in the previous century was recognized by the authorities and,
in the years following, numerous Clearance and Demolition Orders,
particularly after the 1919 Housing Act, were placed on cottages in
the village. Many of those jerry-built ones, squashed into the yards

behind the High Street and Bailey Street, on the Massingham Road and at St James's Green, were already were falling down on their own.

The first council properties were built in 1921: two bungalows on the north side of Town Lane on a site designed to link the two sections of the old village. In 1930 more land in Town Lane was purchased from the Holkham Estate and four houses were built; two were non-parlour types designed for 'working men' with no parlours or bathrooms though with a well in the garden, and two slightly superior ones with a parlour. The earl of Leicester was in favour of these houses being built in Town Lane rather than the Massingham Road; the tenant of the field behind complained of damage done during the building work and, later, his cattle strayed into the gardens. The houses were not built by local men, as had historically been the case, but by Hammond Brothers of West Lynn. One of the parlour type houses was leased to Mr Crowther, Schoolmaster from 1930-1939. Originally Mr Everington of Lodge Farm, a School Governor, had proposed, and Norfolk County Council had agreed, to build a house specifically for the Schoolmaster, but it was doubted the plans would receive a Government grant; which may explain the building of the parlour types, deemed more suitable for a 'professional man.' Since the time the School was first built in 1838 there had never been a Schoolmaster's house to go with it, nor was this addressed when the School was enlarged in 1873.

Four more Council houses in Town Lane followed in 1933, for which there were thirteen applicants. Further land was bought by the Council for housing at Pye's Lane, where in 1939 an estate of brick houses and bungalows was built and named de Warenne Place, due to its proximity to the Castle. Immediately after the war, and initially put up as a temporary measure but still standing and now in the conservation area due to their rarity, several wooden Swedish houses and

HELEN BREACH

Wooden bungalow in Town Lane

bungalows were built there. A second council estate to the west of the Massingham Road, built post-war, is named Foxes Meadow after the old manor. Many of these houses are now in private ownership.

The Second World War 1939-45 was the cause of more direct change in the village than the first had been. The depression in the late 1920s and 30s had already seen many leave the village in search of work elsewhere and when and if they came back it was often with wives, or husbands, from 'away'. Young women went to work in domestic service in London, finding jobs there through a network of contacts. The war was to expand horizons further. Village girls took jobs in Swaffham canning vegetables and for the first time enjoyed some real independence. Land girls arrived from other parts of England. Airmen and soldiers abounded. Italian prisoners of war cleaned out the Nar and the drains that ran into it; several of them and a sizeable number of Germans remained in Norfolk when the war ended. Agriculture, too, changed out of all recognition with the first tractors in the 1940s and the demise of the horse. The first woman was elected onto the Parish Council and the Women's Institute paid for the village sign on Stocks Green.

Eventually running water, electricity, television and the motor car appeared. By the 1970s Holkham had sold almost all the properties it owned in the village though it retained and still retains two of the farms, the Manor and the Lodge. The Wicken Farm was sold to the tenant Mr Keith in 1955. In the 1970s, executive houses were built along Back Lane, once Swinesgate; meanwhile several of the remaining old cottages were bought as holiday or week-end homes. When Conservation areas were set up in 1971 Castle Acre was one of the first three villages in Norfolk chosen. As a result a detailed conservation plan of how the village should be improved was made and this led to more clearances of cottages on the High Street and the building of new ones. Later the Conservation area was extended north to St James's Green and east to include the wooden Swedish Council houses built in 1947 on de Warrene Place. More new homes were built in North Street at the end of the 1970s.

The field at the back of Town Lane was given to the village by the earl of Leicester in 1977 for a Playing Field, which it still is, well used and enhanced in the year 2000 with a new children's playground and skate-boarding area.

A sewage works was constructed on the water meadows in the 1980s designed to work on the soak-away system, but for reasons of landfall was not able to serve all the houses in the village. When Anglian Water threatened to solve the problem by directing the overflow into the Nar the village protested and made the national papers the day a symbolic 'Synchronised Flush' was arranged. The village

81

won and the soak-away was extended. This encouraged more new building in the village, a development on Pales Green in the 1990s and since then many more new houses, mainly infilling, somewhat reminiscent of the nineteenth-century speculators.

Recently another battle has been fought and won when a public inquiry was held to determine the rights and wrongs of filling a nearby quarry with toxic waste. Today in the twenty-first century the commons have largely reverted to wilderness, the river continues to be periodically choked with weeds, parking problems have largely replaced muck on the streets and unringed swine, but the school is full, the remaining shops and pubs flourish, tourists flock and people greet each other in the street.